What Do Communities Have?

by Cynthia Swain

I need to know these words.

building

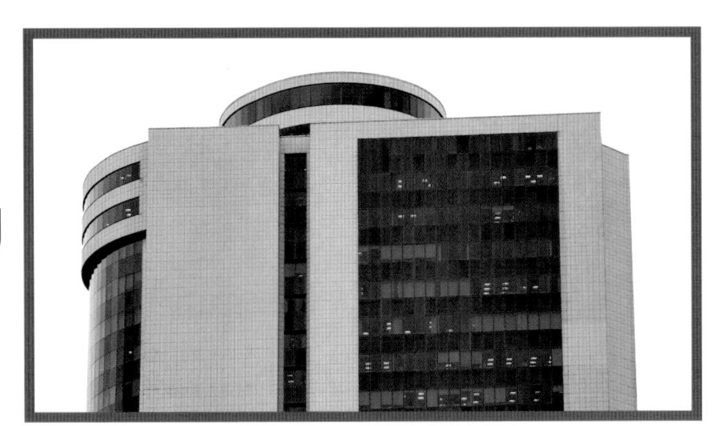

bus

house

people

I see a **house**.

8404

I see a store.

GENERAL STORE
OLD FASHIONED STUFF
Summer Sizzlers
ANTIQUES
collectibles
Summer Sizzlers
CLOSED
CLOSED
SALE

I see a **bus**.

18A NICOLLET-46
SAVE MORE THAN THE PRICE OF GAS.
LEARN HOW AT METROTRANSIT.ORG
Go GREENER
Hybrid
Electric Bus
7122
GREENER
Go GREENER
Hybrid
Electric Bus

I see a horse.

I see a school.

I see a **building**.

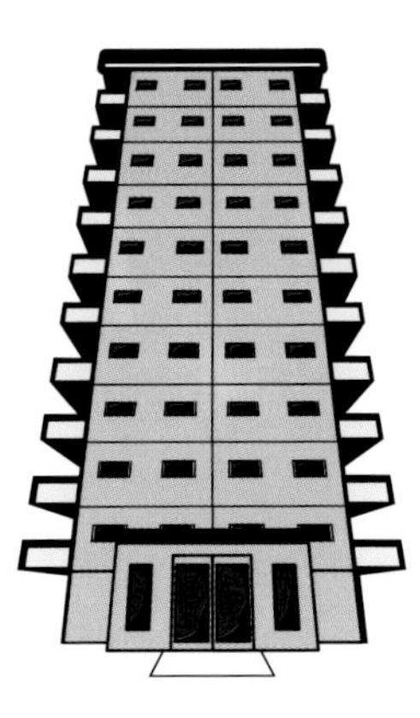

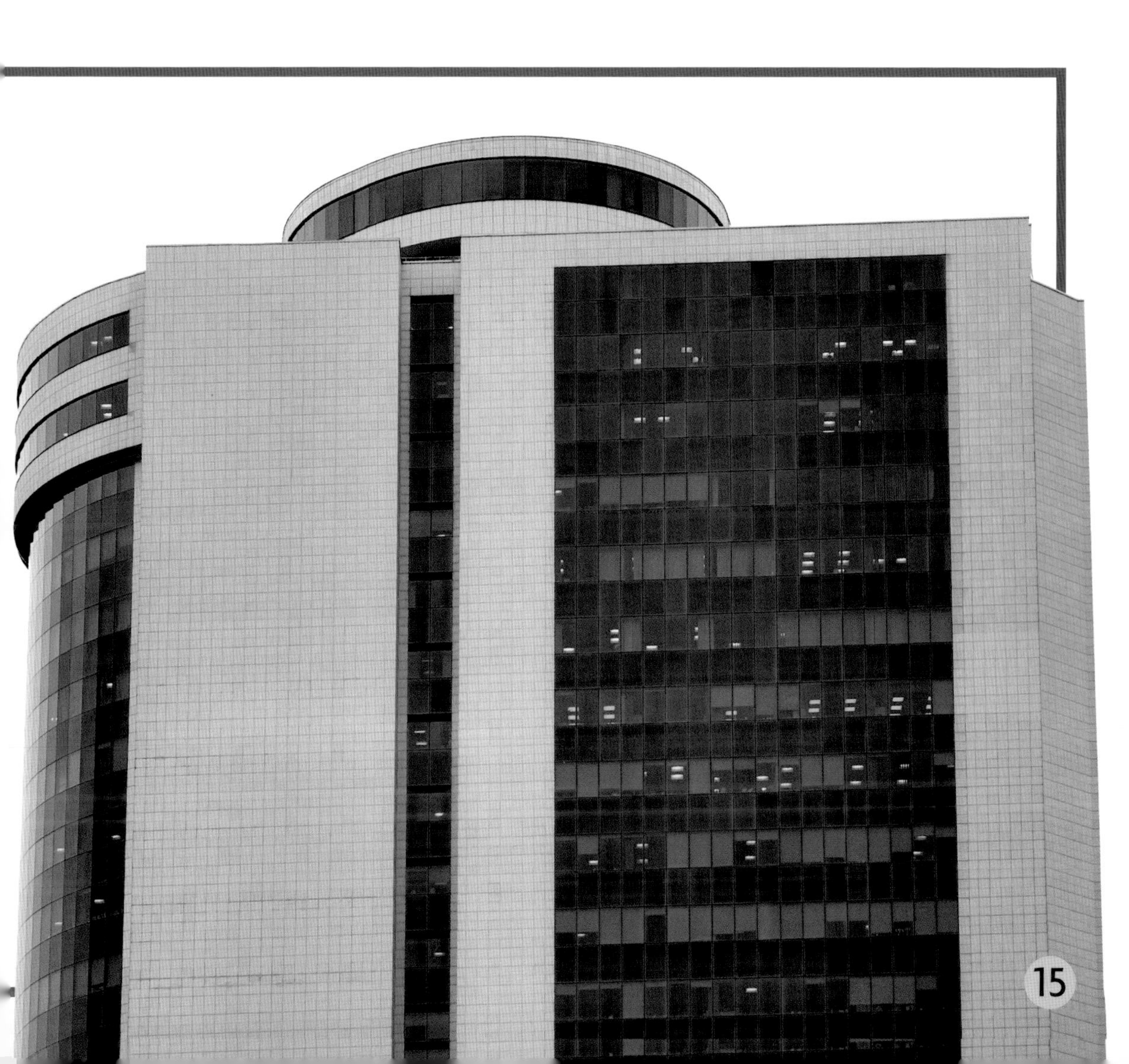

I see **people.**